THE LITTLE B

DRAGONS

FINDING YOUR SPIRIT GUIDE

Christine Arana Fader

With illustrations by
Anja Kostka

EARTHDANCER

AN INNER TRADITIONS IMPRINT

First Edition 2015, reprinted 2020
The Little Book of Dragons – Finding Your Spirit Guide
Christine Arana Fader

This english edition © 2015 Earthdancer GmbH
English translation and editing: JMS Books LLP, www.jmswords.com

Originally published in German as *Das kleine Drachenhandbuch*
World copyright © 2014 Schirner Verlag, Darmstadt, Germany

Cover: Simone Fleck, Schirner, using # 57586834
by nj_musik, and # 52670792 by JohanSwanepoel,
both www.fotolia.com
Illustrations: Anja Kostka

Typesetting and graphic design: Dragon Design
Typeset in Minion

Printed and bound in Canada by Marquis

ISBN 978-1-84409-670-1 (print)
ISBN 978-1-84409- 830-9 (ebook)

Published by Earthdancer, an imprint of Inner Traditions
www.earthdancerbooks.com, www.innertraditions.com

CONTENTS

FOREWORD

I now know that dragons have been with me since the beginning of time – they are travelling companions that I could never be without. Their love and loyalty touch me deep within my heart. The first time in this life that I looked deep into the eyes of a dragon, I was so moved, I couldn't hold back the tears and I fell to my knees – I saw the unending love of the divine source within. There's a touch of magic to the strength you feel when a dragon stands behind you to protect you and strengthen your resolve. You don't have to bathe in its blood, like Siegfried did in the Middle High German heroic epic *Nibelungenlied* (Song of the Nibelungs). Connect with your dragon heart to heart and the spark of invincibility will spring to you. There are many legends telling of dragons and the gigantic hoards of precious stones that they guard, but in such stories, it's not piles of gems that dragons are watching over, it's knowledge. Knowledge is power, and only those who are pure in heart should gain access to this knowledge. The world is in flux, the rule of fear is faltering, and, just as it was at the beginning, love will return to rule at the end – that much is certain. Many movies and novels, and every fairytale, all tell us so, and they all recount the same story: the story of love and its victory over fear.

The dragons and the dragon riders are returning. You may well think that they are the stuff of legends and indeed they are, but who's to say that legends aren't true? We humans have often been wrong, believing something to be true only to discover that the reality is quite different. We think we are so superior and so knowledgeable, but believe me, we know very little. It is up to us if legends come true, it is up to you to become the hero of your own legend, your own story. I'm going to tell you one of the great truths – you know it already of course… but I will tell it to you anyway: every war is won in the heart.

And now I shall tell you another great truth – knowing this is not enough. Only when your knowledge transforms into wisdom will you be able to make use of the truth – then peace will rule in your heart, and when peace rules in all our hearts, we will have peace in every part of the world. Old values are returning with the dragons – values such as courage, loyalty, true friendship, companionship, the knowledge that you are not alone. Heed the call and bring your dragon back – it has been waiting for you for millions of years. Reach out to it heart to heart, absorb this great, endless love deep within yourself and use it to bring about peace on this our Earth, on Lady Gaia, your great mother, who bears you and nourishes you each day.

THE DRAGON –
A POWER ANIMAL

A dragon is a spark of the celestial source that carries the divine fire, come to life. It stands for the magical power of the universe and is the guardian of magic, of the elements and their power, and of yin and yang, which keep life on our Earth in equilibrium. Dragons live in reality – where they belong as guardians of magical knowledge. Magic is knowledge of knowledge. Magic is the most natural thing on Earth. Magic is everything that entrances you. Magic is when you plant a sunflower seed in the soil and a tall, magnificent sunflower grows from it. Magic is when I tell you how wonderful you are and bring a smile to your face. Magic surrounds us – it is everywhere. It is ethereal, flooded with light and powerful. Dragons are magical and have always existed. They were present at the creation of our galaxy, at the time they were charged with their task. They are older than all the planets, older than any soul. They have a direct line to the source of all existence. This alone is the reason we experience feelings of such awe at the sight of a dragon, or perhaps even a slight frisson of fear – we fear its power, a feeling from our collective unconscious.

Being powerful has negative associations for many, but that need not be the case. It is only negative when power is abused. Dragons are pure love. Those hungry for power have said 'bad' things about them, knowing that dragons endow their companions with power and magical knowledge, which in turn means that people can live their lives independently and free of fear – powerful people have wanted to prevent this. Dragons are returning to the present day. It is their wish and that of the spiritual world that we live a life of love, independent and free from fear. We all have the same power. Others are more powerful than us because they steal our power.

If a dragon touches you, it wishes to teach you to take up the place that has been prepared for you. It will put you in touch with great forces and teach you to command the power of the elements. It is the guardian of the entire knowledge of the universe. It will teach you to follow your own path with courage, and to grow beyond yourself. Your dragon will tell you that lazy compromises must come to an end. It wants you to raise yourself up from a lower plane to a higher one, to accept your destiny and your duties, as every task accomplished brings you closer to mastery, closer to your spiritual plan.

This is the path along which the dragons wish to lead us. The path is not smooth, it's not easy to pick our way along what can be a lonely and stony road, but only this path will lead us into the light and to freedom.

The souls that are given a dragon as a companion are the oldest of the old, the guardians, the magicians and the high priestesses since the beginning of time. Those who see dragon riders in themselves are ready to look into the mirror of truth, to accept themselves and the great task once given them. The unconscious has magical powers and can lead us in mystical ways. Trust your dragon and trust your heart. Do so at all times, at every moment and with every breath. There are many different kinds of dragons and I would like to introduce you to some of them in this book, but first, follow the trance journey described to find your dragon. Then you can devote yourself to the task he sets you. Everything I write about dragons in this book is, of course, a generalization, but there is something entirely individual in every encounter with a dragon, every connection between a human being and a dragon is unique. To connect other people with their dragons, read the trance journey to them.

Find yourselves, so you can work with your dragon – you have been companions of the heart since the beginning of time.

MY FIRST DRAGON
AND HOW IT ALL BEGAN

I attended my first spiritual workshop in Hamburg in 2000 and it was there that I came to enjoy several profound and extremely well-led trance journeys. On one of these journeys, the goal was to make contact with your heart. However, for me, the journey took a rather different turn. Where my heart should have been, I found a giant egg. As I inspected it a little more closely, I noticed there was something moving inside and through the faintly transparent shell I thought I could see scales. My mind was racing, I thought, 'If a snake jumps out of that, I will have a complete fit.' We had been told to place our heart where it belonged. Heavens, what was I supposed to do? So I picked up the egg and swallowed it; I really couldn't think of anything better to do at the time. At first I thought it wouldn't be possible, as the egg was so big, but somehow I managed it. My whole body flushed with heat, sweat beaded on my forehead and I could feel something alive in my chest. I had a slight feeling of rising panic. As I looked down at my chest, the skin on the left side over my heart opened up. My panic increased, but then a tiny red dragon slipped out and my panic gave way to fascination. The dragon shone with a fiery red light and I fell in love with it at first sight. Without understanding what was happening, my heart exploded with a deep love. At the time, as I have said, I knew little of spiritual things, let alone of power animals or spirit guides. The sight of a small red dragon touched my heart and I felt a strong connection and a very deep love. It scrabbled over my shoulder and down my arm, wrapped its tail around my wrist, poked the arrow-shaped tip of its tail into a vein on the inside of my left forearm, laid its little head on the back of my hand, closed its eyes and went to sleep. I looked at it closely – it looked cute and was fast asleep. As I looked at my wrist, I suddenly noticed on my ring finger a gold band that looked like a wedding ring. This puzzle was to be solved only many years later.

Once I got back home, I started making trance journeys almost every day and all the things I experienced would fill another, extremely thick book – but this one is about dragons.

In addition to the small red dragon, I acquired another guide. Once I returned home from Hamburg, an angel began to appear in my sitting room every evening. At first I was very reverential and didn't dare speak to him, but after a while I plucked up the courage. He introduced himself as the Archangel Uriel. As I had not heard of such an angel, I had to do some research and looked him up on the internet.

Uriel became my teacher. On one of the trance journeys, I asked him what was the meaning of the small red dragon. He answered: 'It represents the magic you carry within you.'

On each of these trance journeys, I noticed the dragon on my wrist; it was always there. As I went about my everyday life, I could sometimes feel its little head resting peacefully on the back of my hand. I'm not exactly sure, but I think I carried my sleeping dragon about on my wrist for around three years, connected to me and the blood circulating through my body by the arrow-shaped tip of its tail inserted into my vein.

Over the course of these three years, I underwent intensive training – I became a lightworker, I was initiated, and the knowledge that I had carried within for several incarnations was revealed to me slowly and gradually. Uriel showed me a great deal; he showed me the Akasha Chronicle, and he taught me concentration and stamina. He also taught me that love is the most powerful force in the universe.

I would like to share with you two lessons that I found extremely valuable. They would always begin in the same way: I would light some sage incense in the room and pray and dance, then I would sit down quietly on the sofa and close my eyes. Uriel usually took me to a birch wood infused with light for the lessons, but on one particular occasion he did not. This time, I remained in my sitting room. Suddenly, I noticed a small monster standing in the corner of the room, and then a second one in another corner. In just a few seconds many monsters were in the room. They all looked different; some were large, some small, but they all had one thing in common: they all looked horrible.

Some had suppurating sores on their heads, others had an eye hanging out. I was gripped and paralysed by a terrible fear and whimpered softly, 'Uriel, help me!'

Then a path opened up between all the monsters and I was engulfed in white light and blinded. Uriel stepped out of the light and looked down at me as his words thundered out: 'How small you are, that you can't love something simply because you find it ugly.' The words cut me to the quick, penetrating deep into my heart. Uriel turned to one of the monsters and motioned it to come forwards. It was small, green and slimy, with huge, round eyes that were staring at me. Uriel said, 'Take a good look, this is your monster. It is your fear of having to die alone. It belongs to you and is a part of you. Are you unable to love it because it is ugly?' I looked at the monster, and then I saw a fat tear welling up in the huge round eyes of this horrendous creature. I began to sob and cried out loudly to the room, 'I love you all, I love you!' Not one of the monsters looked any different, but instead I was the one who had changed – I was able to look at them and love them, and they all lost their ugliness. Every single monster was beautiful and worth being loved. Uriel was smiling at me.

I am so grateful to him because this was one of the most valuable lessons I learned and I will never forget it. I jumped up from the sofa, pulled on my shoes and shouted: 'All you monsters, get in my car, we're going dancing!' We drove to a club together and danced the whole night away.

Months passed and then one evening Uriel brought the Archangel Michael with him. He introduced us and said Michael would be teaching me over the next few weeks. The teaching consisted of learning to control my thoughts. I was a terrible pupil. With Michael, I was usually not allowed to sit down, so one evening I found myself on my feet in my sitting room, once again tasked with concentrating, but my thoughts would not stop wandering. I had been really annoyed with someone at the office that day and was unable to focus my thoughts within the room. Michael, who was standing opposite me, spoke, saying, 'Get out of your head and into your heart. Get out of your head and into your heart!' His words became more and more insistent, but I kept failing. And then it happened: as quick as a flash, he drew his sword and chopped off my head. I saw my head roll across the floor, right in front of my spiritual eye, while physically this 'vision' knocked my head to one side with great force. Michael stretched out his hands in front of him and fashioned a new head for me out of light. I will never forget this lesson either, as it was extremely painful physically and for the next two weeks I walked around with a stiff and sprained neck.

In this lesson, I learned that we have to keep our thoughts in check when we begin to rediscover our magic and thus our power, since our thoughts are powerful. Other people pick up on our bad thoughts, and just because we are angry, we shouldn't send out bad vibrations to that person. This is also what is meant when we say, 'All wars are won in the heart.'

From Michael, I learned that sometimes we have to fight to keep the peace and he taught me that on occasion we must let go to follow our own path. At times, both can be painful and not enjoyable, and occasionally frightening, but they strengthen us and give us courage. A wonderful teacher once asked me: 'Who is that represents courage? To which person would you attribute such resonance? It is Jesus Christ. He stands for courage, and the courageous ones amongst us are his disciples ... always and at any time.'

The years flew by. One day, with Uriel once again at my side, I was undergoing my trance journey to my place of inner strength, as I always did, and naturally glanced down at my wrist, as was my habit. Full of love, I thought, 'How sweetly it sleeps, my small red dragon.' Suddenly, it opened its eyes – after more than three years, just like that! I could hardly believe it. I stared at the dragon, petrified. And it wasn't just because it had opened his eyes, it was moving as well. It withdrew the arrow-shaped tip of its tail from my vein. A few drops of blood ran down my arm and fell to the ground as if in slow motion. The small wound closed up in front of my eyes as if by magic, leaving a tiny scar. I leaned forward to allow the small red dragon to hop down from my hand, and before it had even reached the ground it began to grow in size and became enormous. I shrank back, scarcely able to believe what was happening. It then turned its now huge head towards me and I looked into its shining, dark-brown eyes. What I could see there touched me so deeply that tears flowed down my cheeks. For what I saw was love. I approached the dragon with my arms flung wide and leaned against its chest. I was so happy. It became my constant companion for many years.

In 2004 I moved to Frankfurt, and my dragon naturally came with me and discovered its passion for metro tunnels. We were united in a deep love. Every evening as I went to bed, it would look out for me, making deep gurgling noises, sniffing over my duvet and sitting back contentedly when it saw that everything was fine. Sometimes it slept curled up in front of my bed. Yes, it was possible – there was only room for its snout, but that didn't matter: there is no material world for dragons as there is for us; the wall of the house didn't exist for my dragon.

I experienced many things with my big red dragon: it showed me the interior of Lady Gaia. We slipped through the magma chambers of this world together, the greatest places of power that I know. Bright red magma, as red as my dragon. Occasionally we would fly up to the stars, to enjoy the most beautiful view in existence: our Earth, the blue planet. Seeing Lady Gaia in her overwhelming beauty and entirety always moves me to tears.

From my great red dragon I have learned what beauty really means: that it is eternal and always connected with love. It has filled my heart with peace and given me irresistible strength. Our parting took place in 2008 and was dreadful. I cried for weeks. I don't want to go into the details, as I don't know how I can explain it. But there is one thing that I would like to say: the dragon gave its life to save mine.

The dragon was my friend, my love, my saviour.

My conscience tormented me for months. Was it my fault? I know now that it was the dragon's task and that it was for this reason alone that it had come to me. I know now that the queen herself had sent the dragon to protect me, so that nothing and no one could come between me and my own task. Today, the dark side trembles before me in fear; I am free of fear and stronger than ever before.

A few months after I lost my red dragon, I began to think that it was time for a new power animal. As I didn't trust myself – my yearning for my red dragon was too great – I booked an appointment with a spiritual teacher to find a power animal. In retrospect, this appointment proved much more worthwhile than I had initially anticipated. The teacher took me in a trance to another world. I followed the path before me and came to a great lake, a lake that drew me towards it magically. I knew instinctively that I had to enter it, and so I went in and looked down to the bottom.

There I saw an old black dragon. It was held captive, deep down on the bed of the lake. When I found it, it was weak and bound by thick chains to the rock under the water. I was horrified at the sight. It lay motionless before me, the broad iron rings with their heavy locks pressing deep into the flesh of its legs. I felt a rage growing inside me. Who would do such a thing, and how could I free the dragon? My thoughts raced through my head. 'I have no key', I kept thinking, 'I can't open these locks – I have no key!' But my strength grew with my anger, and then an idea came into my head, calm yet powerful: I don't need a key! Something flooded through me; I knelt down on the lake bed, stretched out my hands and touched the manacles on its feet. A single touch of my hand was enough for the chains to crumble to dust. The dragon's wounds were deep and I could see a hole in its left wing. I brought it to the shore and told it that it could recover there. At that moment I was unaware that this black dragon was my spiritual companion.

The dragon stayed behind at the lake, weakened, but free. I left, still searching for my power animal. As I departed, I looked down and saw that I was wearing a long, dark blue dress, very simple and quite old. I was also wearing sandals and a grey cape. They were not the clothes I had been wearing when I entered the lake to help the dragon. In the far distance I could see a white stag, looking at me. Something familiar stirred in my heart, a vague memory, a recollection of a fateful encounter. I returned from my trance journey to the room in which I had been sitting with this white woman.

We opened our eyes and she looked at me and said, 'You belong in Avalon.'

For several weeks after I returned home, I tried to bring the white stag closer to me; I thought it would be my new power animal. Of course, I didn't succeed because it was not my power animal, it was a memory of another time. But I didn't understand the significance then.

The black dragon recovered and came to me. At first, I wasn't very happy that the dragon was now at my side as it was silent and a little frightening, but we slowly made friends. I was astonished when I learned just what the rider of a black dragon's task is. My black dragon wears a golden halter and reins. But I also felt a deep connection between our hearts.

We have been connected for several years now, and I can't imagine life without my black dragon (his name is simply Black). My life has changed with Black, and I have grown with his presence in my aura. He has brought happiness, peace and fulfilment into my life. We are a team that unites Man and Dragon. Black is the spiritual guide that the source placed at my side when my soul was created. At that moment, I was charged with a task, a task that lies beyond illusion. It is my soul's task – Black and I are light-filled warriors in the service of love, until the end of time and perhaps even beyond.

BLACK

And so I connected, heart to heart, with my spiritual guide, to renew an old alliance, and since then he has shown me the path once more. Black has brought me to the mirror of truth that stands in the golden temple of the sun god, so that I can recognise myself. I see myself as a woman with long black hair, a black dress and a broad, heavy sword with a golden handle. The old brown leather belt from which my sword hangs is much too big for me. I know that I am keeping the sword safe for a warrior until he returns to fight at my side for love. Beneath the dress I am wearing tight trousers and there are no shoes on my feet. I can clearly see the wedding ring that I have been wearing on my left ring finger since I gave birth to the little red dragon from my heart.

It is thanks to Black that I have been able to write this little book of dragons, and he has also enabled me to renew my connection with Merlin, hence my book A *Conversation with Merlin*. The first dragon workshops began after that. Black never strayed from my side. The dark side tried to attack me several more times, but with a shadow hunter at my side and with my new, unwavering, light-filled strength, it was no longer able to frighten me. A female medium once

told me: 'You should always expect the dark side to try to attack you. If you are living to your full potential, you have the power to proclaim the end of the rule of fear, so that the rule of love – and thus the golden age – may return.' I am no longer scared.

You can lead a life without meaning for many years – it is up to you to decide to change that. I reached a point where I decided to do something and be someone meaningful. It may be a small seed now, but in a hundred years it might grow into a mighty tree. I want to do what I can to return this world to the Garden of Eden it once was. Black has shown me the world of dragons. First he took me to the dragon king, Oisin, a brown giant and the oldest of the dragons. Oisin is the first. I recognised pure goodness and the endless love of the divine source in the dragon king's brown eyes. Journeys to see him were always amazing. Oisin generally didn't speak to me, I was simply present. He showed me his holy emerald, the hallowed spring near his cave, and after a few months allowed me to follow the golden path of initiation. This was a great gift. I would often simply stand in the middle of the great square in front of the king's cave, surrounded by hundreds of dragons.

They came and went. It was as if all the dragons wanted to see me. A great number bowed before me and I saw a spark of power in the eyes of many. It was an exciting time. After a while, the dragon queen Alba came to me and invited me to visit. She arrived during a terrible storm – I was driving along the motorway, with hailstones slamming down onto my car. Full of fear, I cried out loudly: 'Black, I need you now.' I sensed him low over the car. Suddenly the dark blanket of clouds tore apart and I saw a large white dragon, sparkling and shining in the sky. I heard her voice in my head, but I have unfortunately forgotten what she said. Black then brought me to her; this journey was so magical and entrancing! Alba is as white as freshly fallen snow and she sparkles and glitters in the light. She is the bearer of such a high vibration of love that it took my breath away for a moment. The love that Alba embodies is something we have forgotten here on Earth. We know the word and we use it, but what we feel is just a tiny part of what is possible. She gave me hope that I can manage to change something, to bring the love of dragons to people, to leave something behind for a new world of peace in the future… I am not exactly sure how, but Black and I have time, if not in this life, then in another. There is no question of giving up.

My love for Black became ever stronger, which enabled him to have increasing influence in my life in the here and now. I would like to recount what is probably the most amazing story. I swear every word is true and this is exactly how it happened.

Around 7pm on a beautiful and warm summer evening, I was standing at some pedestrian lights on a three-lane road, waiting for them to turn green so that I and several other people could cross. In all, there were five other people standing there, two beside me and three on the opposite side of the road. We were all staring at the red man symbol on the lights. I suddenly sensed Black behind me. He was spreading out his energy to enclose me and all the other people and he was switching us off. It was exactly as though he was pulling a plug. My thoughts raced crazily back and forth through my head. What was happening? The pedestrian light went green and no one moved. Everybody stood as if paralysed, looking at the green man. Suddenly, a car shot through the lights, greatly exceeding the speed limit. Black withdrew his energy and everyone started to cross. No one said anything; nobody had noticed a thing. No one shouted at the car driver, as would normally happen. They just went silently on their way. Only I stood a little further down the road, gradually realising what I had just experienced…

Black had just possibly saved my life.

Black conjured up memories in me of the time of Avalon and so I wrote my book *Morgaine* in a trance. This book released many things inside me and also healed much within me. I now have a better understanding of some things; I understand myself and my own life. Everything becomes clearer with every breath I take. The circle is closing and yet I am still only at the beginning.

TRANCE JOURNEY

You can find your own personal dragon in the trance journey that follows here. It is best if it is read to you, slowly. Find a suitable place for the journey and light at least one candle. Purify your space by burning some incense (or fragrance of your choice) and put on a CD that helps with meditation and trance journeys, ideally some calming music with no vocals that lasts at least 45 minutes.

If you happen to have a magic stone that you use for other rituals, hold this in your left hand. Arrange a magic protective circle around you, make yourself comfortable, lie down and visualise breathing a blue light. Breathe shining sapphire blue in and out and fill your aura with it. Do this for several minutes. Ground yourself as you always do, perhaps by letting roots grow from your feet deep into the earth. Visualise a column of light rising up out of the earth at your side and flowing off into the eternity of the universe. Be aware that parts of you are going on a journey to meet the dragon that will be your teacher in the near future. It has been your spirit guide since the beginning of time. Slowly, very slowly, release from your body the light-filled part of you, the part that is about to embark upon a journey.

Your face will release itself from your face, your shoulders will detach from your shoulders, your torso will rise, your behind will separate from your behind, and you will stand up. The illuminated parts of you are now standing next to your body. Be aware of this and look at yourself lying there. Your body is protected by the sapphire-blue light or by your magic circle of protection, so don't worry about leaving it behind. Walk into the column of light in the knowledge that you will soon see your dragon. Feel the traction that embraces you and draws you upwards into the column of light. Surrender to this pull. Float upwards, as light as a feather in the wind, surrounded by white light, higher and higher. Lifted aloft as if by hundreds of angel hands. Then take a step beyond the column of light. You are standing in a green valley on a gentle slope and next to your column of light is a tree. Take a close look. What kind of tree is it? Does it have leaves, blossom or perhaps fruit? Look closely at this tree and then down at your feet. Concentrate on them – this is important for your arrival. Feel the ground beneath your feet and let your toes play with the grass. Feel just how firmly you are standing on solid ground. Look around you. See the blue sky above – it is summer.

Now run, descending the gentle hill until you reach a narrow path. Turn left and follow it. It will take you through a valley. A small stream crosses the path, babbling softly; you must jump across to reach the other side. Jump! Keep going. You reach a young wood, full of light.

You enter this beautiful wood, noticing the shafts of light that the warm sun is projecting through the canopy of leaves. You pass an old tree stump that you weren't expecting to find here. Take a look at it. Lightning once hit this ancient, venerable old tree, leaving behind a strange sculpture. A sculpture of God – it is beautiful.

Continue to follow the path; the forest is getting thicker and more ancient. The air in this magical old forest is invigorating and aromatic. Keep going deeper into the forest, never straying from the path. The path suddenly ends at a high rocky wall that rises up above you. Place your right hand on the cool rock and follow the wall along, touching the rock with the fingertips of your right hand. Remind yourself that you are here to meet your dragon. It is already very close. Feel the excitement, the joyful anticipation in your heart. Keep moving along the wall of rock. After a while you reach a small, narrow ravine. High above you, you can see a strip of blue summer sky and in your heart you feel the energy of your dragon. You know you have to climb the rock – roots and projecting stones will help you. Climb up and pull yourself out of the ravine. You are now standing on a high plateau and can see far down into the valley. You can see the path you took, the stream, the tree and the column of light that awaits. Remain standing there, very quietly and peacefully, and look up into the blue sky. Your dragon approaches from behind. Don't turn round, the dragon will reach out to you. Remain standing, calmly, and wait before calling out with your inner voice, 'I am ready!' Repeat these words twice.

Now you feel a hot blast of air behind you, but don't turn round. Concentrate on your heart, let love flow. You can clearly feel the hot breath of your dragon on your back. Stand still calmly. Your dragon is behind you. Feel its presence, its powerful, hot energy. It is standing right behind you, you can feel its heart. Tell it with your inner voice that you are ready. It touches you gently on your right shoulder. This is the sign.

Take a few steps forwards and then turn around. Look at your dragon, its vast size and its powerful aura. Take your time – look at its front legs, its broad chest. Lift your head and examine its head closely. The dragon lowers its mighty head to you and you look into its eyes and recognise the endless love within. This is your dragon, your companion. Feel the deep love between you. Look at it closely, the curve of its neck, its back, its hind legs, its mighty wings.

Walk around your dragon slowly and gaze at it closely to the very tip of its tail.

Now, stand in front of your dragon and look at its chest. See how a silver energy vortex forms there and how a silver, illuminated thread then separates from this vortex and comes towards you. The time has come. Let a silver vortex of energy form in your heart too, and release a silver, light-filled thread from your heart. These two silver threads meet in the space between you, wrap around each other in a spiral and flow into one another. Now spread your heart wide open and take the silver thread of love from the heart of the dragon into yourself. Feel this endless love that is older than all life, a love from a different time, older than Lady Gaia, powerful and pure.

Your dragon opens its heart too and takes the silver thread from your heart into itself. Your love floods into it. Look how it throws back its head, listen to the cry of your dragon. It spreads its wings out for you. Feel your happiness and sense the words in its heart: 'My rider has returned!' No one can break the silver thread of love; you are united for eternity. The bond has been renewed. You both retrieve the silver thread with care and it is time to start the journey back. Say farewell to your dragon for now; take your leave as you wish, with a bow, a hug or even with a kiss.

Go back to the rocky ravine and climb down. It is time to travel back, back, back...

When you have reached the bottom, stretch out your left hand and touch the cool stone of the rock wall. Follow the rocky wall and feel the stone with the fingertips of your left hand. You can see the path in front of you, leading into the dense, ancient forest. Feel the omnipresent magic that surrounds you. The forest now becomes less dense and less ancient, and the path leads back past the old tree stump where lightning once struck. Keep following the path and leave the wood. Follow the path through the green valley, leap over the narrow stream once again and climb the gentle hill to the column of light that awaits you. Look up briefly into the blue summer sky and see how your dragon is gliding high above, majestic, serene and powerful. You are united for all eternity. Now take a step into the column of light and surrender to the force that takes hold of you instantly and drags you back down. Allow yourself to descend, surrendering yourself to the white light. You drift down gently, deeper and deeper, as light as a feather in the wind, surrounded by white light. Step out of the column and return entirely to the here and now, step back into your room. Gently and slowly, return the parts of you that went on the journey back into your body. Feel how they reconnect with your body – your feet and legs have returned and are replacing themselves, feel how your torso is back within your body, how your face, too, is melding back perfectly with your face. Turn your attention to your spine and connect every individual vertebra from bottom to top. Be clearly aware of how they join together, like a zip being closed. Take a few deep breaths, and when you are ready, open your eyes on a new future. A future with a dragon at your side, freed from fear and filled with love, wisdom and MAGIC. It's now up to you what you make of it. It's up to you how much life you breathe into your dragon. Connect with it every day, become inseparable friends. Take it everywhere you go and say goodnight to it every evening when you go to bed. Tell it how much you love it every day and prepare for a life full of miracles.

THE WHITE DRAGON
AIR, LIGHT OR CRYSTAL DRAGON

This dragon is white, mother-of-pearl or translucent in colour. Master of the skies, it shines brightly and possesses an elegant beauty. It brings purification and clarity, its brightness shining into the darkest corners of your being to reveal where your shadows lie. With love and patience, it teaches you to accept those shadows and to integrate them into your life as they are a part of you. Recognise that you are the creator of your shadows. The light dragon illuminates the fear in you and lovingly enfolds you in its wings. Connect with its power and be ready to let go of your fears, so that the power of love can flow right through you and your life. Fear is the opposite of love; wherever fear reigns, there is no place for love, and, in turn, love is the only power that can heal. So, gather your courage and follow this wonderful being. Recognise that it is a part of you and accept this part.

Become a rider of wind and light and recognise your own nature.

To the wise men of our forefathers, the druids and the sorcerers, air was the master element, the most difficult to command, impossible to comprehend – as ineffable as

our spirit and our thoughts. Everything is connected to everything else through the element of air. When you are united heart to heart with a white dragon, when this is an old union freshly renewed, you receive the gift of commanding the element of air. Air is breath, and with every breath your body takes, it is saying yes to life. Your body does this without asking you and normally you don't even think about having to breathe in order to live. Breathing is an act that seems so familiar and unspectacular, but it is nonetheless a miracle. The element of air teaches us how powerful the invisible world is.

The white dragon will take you to the lake of unshed tears within you. Free these tears – allow yourself the time you need to cry and to mourn all that you need to mourn. Use this time of purification. Pay attention to your diet and eat no meat, drink no alcohol and categorically avoid nicotine. Get back to nature and breathe *prana*. Seek out peace and solitude and find the power of your dragon. Cleanse your body by burning incense or sage, and let go of all your tears. When this time has passed, you will shine with the same light as your dragon.

The white dragon will travel with you to all the ancient magical places of power, to the pyramids, the Inca temples, the temples in India, to all the holy places of the world. Learn from it how to feel the power of these places. You are the light that they are missing and need in order to shine again.

It is your task to reawaken these places. Many of the ancient columns of light that once shone out over them were deactivated many years ago, when the rule of love had to surrender to the rule of fear. The white dragon and its riders can reactivate these columns of light. When your heart is free of tears, it will take just a single touch of your hand. The same is true of all holy places, and our hearts too are such a place. A single touch brings freedom. So go, and touch hearts that are filled with suffering and exchange the suffering for love.

A white and a black dragon are often seen together; their riders are companions from a long-lost time. They are united in their purpose: the ascent of Lady Gaia. Should there be a black dragon rider of the opposite sex in your area, meet with them. You may need their assistance in activating the light columns. Examine maps closely to determine where these old temples and holy places are situated. Meditate with your dragon and fly to these places, but never make the journey without your dragon. Go, and find places where the mightiest light columns on Earth once shone out. Always keep your dragon behind you and connect with it, heart to heart, so that its magical powers can become yours. Lay your hands on the place and speak the following words in a loud and powerful voice: 'I, … (your name), command divine order for this holy place. May the magical power of love shine through me, as I pronounce order for this sacred place. Divine order is restored to this place through the power of magic and the light-filled power of my dragon. Light column, be activated once more – now! So be it.'

During this ritual, let light flow from your hands. Remain at the place for a time, so that you can become charged with power from the column of light. You will need it, as you still have much to do.

When you are deeply connected with your dragon, when you are one, the power that flows from your hands is as powerful as the breath of God.

THE BLACK DRAGON

The black dragon is a fighter and one of the true warriors of the light. Like all dragons, and its human friend, it is peace loving. However, when necessary and to protect others, it is ready and waiting and not afraid to fight. Courageous and selfless, it will battle for the light to the bitter end if required. Although not especially large, the black dragon is extremely quick and agile. Its wings have a wide span, allowing it to glide silently for long periods. Black dragons are shadow hunters; their riders have no fear of shadows. Even if you cannot quite imagine it now, this very power is within your potential, too. When it comes to protecting our planet, you are the one who will face a demon and step up to the fight. The riders of black dragons are ready to go to any lengths to protect our great mother or the queen, or any other who needs protection; but they are also wise and use their great strength judiciously. They are silent warriors; for them, silence has more value than speech. The black dragon and its rider meditate together. They know their gifts, they know the secret of this connection.

41

This team of rider and dragon is devoted to the services of love like no other. The black dragon and its rider possess the ability to dive deep into the world of shadows. They can penetrate into areas that remain hidden from others. When they travel together, they are freed from collective thought, from judgements and condemnations. They recognise everything in its divine truth.

The black dragon will teach you that there is a divine order in the deep silence of your heart, which will lead you to the golden path of your soul and on to your destiny. It will teach you the certainty that there is a divine order in everything and that it is your task to restore or maintain this throughout the galaxy. Meditate with your black dragon and practise flying with it as often as you can. This is not quite as simple as with the other dragons, since black dragons can fly more than three times faster. You will need to work on your reactions, but it is great fun! Your body must be supple, so do some exercises and stretches. Unobstructed energy can only flow through a supple body and only a supple body has the ability to react quickly. The black dragon teaches its riders that it is necessary to give up everything that is superficial and to leave behind any friends who will not follow this path. It teaches that it is sometimes necessary to separate yourself from anything that wants to keep you small.

Take every step with courage. The black dragon teaches that loneliness can sometimes be the price we pay for our path, but that loneliness is certainly not our destiny but merely a temporary section of it along the way. We will find our companions. Those who ride a dragon, those who are courageous – these are the companions who love us, because they understand. Some of the black dragons were once seduced by the dark side. You can recognise them by their head harness woven from gold dust by delicate elfin hands. Elf magic resides in this fine and hair-thin halter and reins and nothing can break them. This delicate harness keeps the dragon in check and tames his wildness. Never remove it but use the knowledge of this dragon to examine the shadows, including your own shadows. Study them; take lying, for example. What is it doing to us? Why do so many people lie? Do you think a person who is free of fear has to lie? Try to understand our addictions, such as drinking and smoking. Why do we damage our bodies? Why don't we love and respect them? Try to understand. Recognise the power of shadows and their many faces. Only one who knows shadows and demons can be a shadow hunter. There are shadows everywhere; understand that only the bright light of love shines powerfully enough to banish what enables the shadows to exist – fear.

THE GOLDEN SUN DRAGON
(ALSO YELLOW OR ORANGE)

The sun dragon will awaken the creator, ruler and magician in you. The sun dragon is mostly encountered as a gold dragon, but all dragons with yellow or orange coloration are sun dragons. It teaches that nothing is impossible. Spend a good deal of time with your sun dragon and activate your power centre. This golden, gleaming dragon is especially large. It invites you to ride on it, on the gleaming light of the sun. The sun was once considered a god by the planet as it created life, and this same characteristic is enjoyed by the sun dragon. It is regal and demands respect. It challenges you to take your place and join the leaders. Don't let people treat you with disrespect.

A king or ruler represents order, clarity and reality, and this is what your dragon teaches. You have a deep connection with the sun god and thus to all sun cultures and their magic. As one who wields the scepter, you bear the *ankh*, the cross of rebirth. It is the symbol of becoming and of dying. The *ankh* is associated with Egyptian culture but is much older. It was first used in Atlantis and bears a deep, long-forgotten magic from that time – a powerful magic from a time when only spiritual people were kings, a time when only the initiated were allowed to rule, for the good of all.

45

Take this dragon to your side and follow the golden path of your soul to your destiny. This wonderful dragon will bring strength, wisdom and beauty into your life. The sun dragon brings together what belongs together and creates a connection between the Spiritual World and human beings. It wants you to find your spiritual partner. When you connect with a sun dragon, your magical power doubles, but when you connect with your spiritual partner and your sun dragon, your shared magical power will be strengthened many times over. You will then be able to achieve miracles together.

When the king and queen follow their golden path together, the land will be fertile. Everything will shine and gleam, as love shall reign. The so-called golden area lies between the solar plexus and the heart chakra. Meditate with your sun dragon; stand before it and ask it to activate this golden area. Approach your sun dragon and lay your breast on its breast. Concentrate on your golden area, between the solar plexus and the heart. Ask your dragon to transfer energy and feel how hot energy flows into you. Feel how all the rigidity and hardening in this area are softened and give way to the power of the sun. Feel how every structure preventing you from being the person that you are dissolves, and feel the power of the dragon in you. The sun dragon teaches you to be wise and to use all your powers with prudence and wisdom. Always remember that you should not interfere with the experiences desired by another soul without permission.

Meditate again with your sun dragon and travel with it to the sun. It will take you to a sun temple in which many secrets are hidden. Take your time, and when you reach it, observe the temple. Be aware of yourself in these surroundings. It is in the sun temple that you will find the mirror of truth. Stand before the mirror and see how you look when stripped of all illusion. See how you are in 'reality'. See how you really look when you leave behind all artifice, when you expand the power of the creator within you. The mirror can also reveal your task. See how much you can do when you become the creator of your life and take this image deep into your heart. Connect daily with this wonderful dragon and become the king or queen, the magician or high priest that you are and have always been.

In the temple of the sun god lives an ancient, golden dragon whose name is ESSSHRAH. It is the dragon of the sun god RA. ESSSHRAH is gigantic in size. When he flies, you see that his wings are flames and his body is covered in large, golden scales. This dragon bears the energy of the origin of all life within it. He can also connect you with this energy, but you cannot call ESSSHRAH – he will come to you and your dragon when you are ready for this vibration. When you are as strong as your dragon and you and your dragon are truly as one, ESSSHRAH will appear. He will then lead you and your dragon to your source and to the spiritual task you were given when your soul was created.

THE SILVER MOON DRAGON

The silver moon dragon brings with it the energy of the moon. It represents the principle of the feminine and expectant, which relies on divine leadership. The silver moon dragon loves the night and the full moon. It is closely acquainted with the power of the moon and teaches you to use this power in your rituals. However, it also teaches that the night of the new moon belongs to the dark side of being, and no rituals are carried out on this night. The silver moon dragon shows you the respect due to all that exists and reveals that there is nothing that does not have the right to exist. An understanding of this indicates you are turning knowledge into wisdom. The moon dragon awakens the priest or priestess in you and will travel with you to Avalon, the isle of apples. It is also the guardian of the secret knowledge of beauty, the Venus within you. Beauty is a gift of creation and is given to us all. The silver moon dragon enables you to see that beauty is eternal, knowing neither time nor space, and is found in everything that has been touched by God's breath. Understand that there is no such thing as time. This gentle dragon teaches you to allow events to occur and take their course without rash interference. It teaches trust. You learn not to be divisive or to judge. Understand that we live in a dual world and that it is important to be unambiguous, but not biased. The wisdom

of the moon dragon is the wisdom of the moon goddess. It guards the knowledge that only by accepting both good and bad, both ends of the scale, can the whole be created. Accept that there is light and darkness in this world and let the wisdom of your dragon flow through you.

A moon dragon rider is devoted to the service of the moon goddess and is thus anointed with the power of the element water, with the flowing, soft aspect of water and its untamed force and life-giving energy. Water is the cradle of life and of healing. The human soul is reflected in the depths of water and can see itself there. You are blessed with this magical creature. Give your dragon all your love and your yearning. This will nourish it and awaken your dragon to an ever greater life.

Follow your dragon into the world of your ancestors and look upon your sometime priests and priestesses. See the beings that stand behind you, the beings that you were in the past. Take this magic and this knowledge back, deep into your heart, and speak to those who need your words just as you used to, full of wisdom and meekness.

The moon dragon is sensitive to light and avoids the glare of the sun. It likes coolness and loves the night. Travel with it to the stars, and let yourself fall. Surrender completely and see what happens when you do nothing, when you think nothing, when you just are, so that your heart can then rise up and overflow with humility. Immerse yourself in the silver light of the moon and become the priest or priestess that you are and always were. The moon dragon will initiate you into the secrets and portals of the twilight. It will show you the crossing places into other dimensions and reveal not just the place but also the time – the right moment. The moon dragon is at the height of its powers at the moment when night touches day and nothing is concealed from it. Meditate with this wonderful dragon and connect to it with your third eye. It wants to teach you to perceive what cannot be seen with physical eyes. Have patience, for it can take time. Stroll with your dragon at dusk, outside in the wild. Go to a stream. Ask your dragon for a small pebble and then search for it in the stream; let your heart guide you. When you have found the pebble, take it in two fingers and hold it in front of your third eye. Connect with the moon dragon and ask it to fill this stone with its power in order to open your third eye.

Then, carry out the following exercise at home: place the small pebble on your third eye and ask the silver moon dragon for support. Listen to beautiful music, look up at the ceiling and roll your eyes clockwise, as if you were trying to draw a great circle with your gaze. Do this exercise for seven minutes.

When you have finished, close your eyes and relax, then repeat the exercise twice more. Alternatively, do the exercise with a small, uncut diamond. When your third eye awakens, remember that the first thing you will 'recognise' is yourself. Turn your gaze within yourself. It is only on the night of a full moon, when your silver dragon will sparkle and gleam in its magical light, that you will be able to see the azure shimmer of your dragon's aura. Then your dragon will shine with its full vibration and strength, deeply connected with the divine source of all existence. Enter the pale blue light of your dragon, lay your forehead against its own and with your inner voice ask for divine order for you, your body and your spirit. Say loudly and clearly: 'Thy will be done through me.' Feel how the pale blue, cool light streams into you through your third eye and fills you completely.

THE RED EARTH OR
FIRE DRAGON

The great fire dragon is surely the dragon that loves people the most. It has a deep connection with us and also with Mother Earth. Its special power is not its ability to fly, but rather that it can take you down into the bowels of the Earth, gliding into the magma. You will find incredible beauty there, bright, shining magma in many shades of red, warm and soothing, relaxing the body. This is your dragon's gift. It puts you in touch with your body. The dragon wants to teach you to respect your body. The body is the temple of the soul and also its expression. The red fire dragon wants to remind you that you are responsible for this temple, that you must look after it, and nourish and protect it. The dragon wants to teach you that only a healthy and supple body really feels good and is open to healing energies. It teaches that feeling and sensing are forms of intuitive knowledge. If your feelings are blocked or clogged with past suffering and pain, or abuse and anxieties that you have experienced, your access to mystical knowledge is also barred to you. Ask your dragon to free you from all your negative experiences and the 'baggage' they have left behind. Open every channel and glide through the magma, the blood of Lady Gaia. Let everything go and receive healing.

The wellbeing of the Earth is equally precious to the red dragon – it communicates with our planet and wants to teach us to understand Lady Gaia as well. It will bring vitality and grounding and it will show you what the material side of life, spiritual rebirth, spiritual strength and spiritual growth really are. As a creature that likes physical affection, it needs your attention, to be touched and caressed. The fire dragon always comes to you just before you fall asleep and nudges you a gentle 'Goodnight'. It guards your dreams and your sleep. It loves places like subway tunnels, underground parking areas, railway stations and of course caves. As the red dragon is often the first dragon to reveal itself, it is ideal for 'dragon beginners'. A family- and child-friendly dragon, it is rather like a dragon version of a Labrador dog. It always likes to be involved and will protect the house and garden and all other pets. Go with the fire dragon through the streets of your town and seek to connect with it, from heart to heart and root chakra to root chakra. Connect yourself to the dragon with a hot, red thread, as hot and warming as Lady Gaia's magma. Then try to see everything around you through its eyes and recognise the beauty that is there. Change the way you look at things; don't just look at what doesn't please you, see what is truly beautiful – even if it is only a tuft of grass pushing up through the asphalt on a road. Kneel before this tuft of grass and see the love of God within it. See the magic of Nature – and of your nature as well. Wherever the love of God reveals itself, beauty is also always to be found. This is the law, the law of creation, and you are a part of it. The fire dragons are old and full of goodness. As the guardians of the country, people and animals, kings and politicians are often accompanied by such a dragon. King Arthur of Britain had a red fire dragon companion.

THE GREEN EMERALD DRAGON

The green emerald dragon loves forests. It finds enclosed spaces hard to bear and has a horror of being confined, too. For this reason, never put a harness or anything similar on this creature that so loves freedom. If an emerald dragon enters your life, conduct a heart meditation with it. Visualise a silver thread connecting you both, between your heart and the dragon's, and you will need neither halter nor reins. The emerald dragon wants to show you the place in your heart where everything precious lies concealed. Open up this place and you will be free, free from fear. The dragon will help you in your search for truth and support you in discovering your truth and the source of insight and understanding in your heart. This beautiful dragon bears three emeralds in its jaws, arranged in order. These holy stones were once given to it by an elven king and were embedded in its mouth as a symbol of its great healing vibration. The emerald dragon knows everything about the healing power of the forest and of Nature. Should you feel unwell, take a trance journey with your green dragon and see where it leads you. It may show you the exact plant that you need to heal you or a place of regeneration.

Some places have this magical power. The green dragon knows them all. You will find the greatest healing vibration in the Amazon forests, where a vibration creates an environment in which every cell of our bodies can regenerate and revitalise. We shall go on a trance journey there, since the Amazon Basin is a dangerous place in the 'illusion' in which we live. Ask your green dragon if you can touch the holy stones in its mouth. They have a great healing vibration but are also stones of truth. When you touch them, the truth will come forth, including your truth, so consider carefully if you are ready for it. Be wise, and think it through thoroughly. The truth is as sharp as the sword of the Archangel Michael and burns like the fire that your dragon can breathe, and yet it is unavoidable. Look at the truth squarely in the face.

The green dragon teaches the harmony of Nature, its laws and its wonders. It wants to instruct you in the sounds of Nature so that you can go deep into the silence of your heart, and all other noises will grow soft or be blocked out altogether. The dragon wants to heal your heart of all things from the past – entrust it with everything and feel its gentleness and love. It wants to teach you to listen with your heart, to hear the sounds between the sounds. Have patience and be prepared to set aside plenty of time. This will help you in conversations, for example with business partners. It will help you to hear what is not being said; you will hear the vibrations and sounds between the spoken words. You will see their fears and recognize their lies. With your new found standing you can be watchful and attentive, treating everyone with respect, and transform low into higher energy. The love and truth from your heart will be the driving force behind all your actions. Make this pledge and follow the path of your soul. Both your heart and that of your dragon are one. Let dragon power shine out in the temple of your heart. Use this to light up the paths of the hearts of others, so that they may recognise the truth and experience healing.

THE TURQUOISE
ATLANTIS DRAGON

The Atlantis dragon is turquoise, although it is sometimes also encountered with white spots. It is graceful in appearance and movement. It exudes peace and elegance and unites freedom and intelligence within itself, combined with feeling. It loves music, art and all creative expression. This beautiful dragon wants you to recall your incarnation in Atlantis, when it was your companion. You forgot it over time and in subsequent incarnations, which certainly caused it some distress, but dragons do not bear grudges as a matter of principle. It wants to reconnect you with the old knowledge of Atlantis, the wisdom, technology and arts of that time. It wants you to remember the high vibrations of crystals and to have them again in your life. Look to see if your Atlantis dragon bears a great larimar on its underbelly, usually positioned centrally, between its front legs. The stone is lodged between its scales. If you find one, try to access the information stored there, using your throat chakra. Hum a note as you touch the larimar and ask your dragon to pass on the old knowledge to you or to reactivate it within you. Hum the note, and during your meditation go on a journey. Fly with the dragon to Atlantis, and see who you were then and what your work was. What did you do in Atlantis? Continue to hum the note and let the waves

63

and the vibrations wash over you. Take a larimar of your own, place it on your neck or forehead and travel with your dragon to Atlantis, learning from it the wisdom that was once thought lost. You already carry it within you.

Much healing power is to be found hidden in the sea, in its flora and fauna. The Atlanteans knew this and some of them had a special knowledge of the properties of the plants in the sea and of their vibrations. The Atlantis dragon is also aware of this. Conduct a meditation and connect with the dragon via a ray of light from your third eye to its third eye. Remain silent and motionless, and go back into memories of previous times – Atlantis. Glide through the ocean with your dragon and speak to the dolphins. Your Atlantis dragon will take you to the most ancient dolphin families. Glide through the seas with them and learn from them. Hear the song of the dolphins, in whose sounds wisdom is rooted.

Know that the Akasha Chronicle also consists of sound – everything consists of notes and sound.

This graceful dragon wants to teach you how to communicate and speak in front of people without fear, and in so doing help you to devote yourself to another form of self-expression, such as singing or painting. This dragon is vivacious and animated, with a life-affirming nature. It invites you to dance and challenges you to express yourself.

Decide which form of self-expression suits you best; sign up for a painting course or start writing a book, but don't do it for other people, do it for yourself. Keep a diary, for example, and write down your experiences with your Atlantis dragon.

Words are the weapons of a master, so become practised in the words of love. The Atlantis dragon teaches that there is a universal order connecting and flowing through everything, that there are universal laws that will exist for eternity, such as the law of cause and effect.

Remember that you once knew all the secrets of the cosmos. Follow your dragon, rediscover and bring back your ancient knowledge to the here and now, so that it can be used anew for the common good, with a purifying light and an even higher vibration. Trust your dragon; it knows what has to be done and which initiations you still require. It will help you become the being that ennobles your spirit, so that your feelings, thoughts and actions will vibrate in harmony with the divine source.

THE VIOLET AMETHYST DRAGON

The violet amethyst dragon wants to acquaint you with your true spiritual side. It will lead you to belief. It radiates peace and equilibrium. Meditate with the dragon. Sit with it and be aware of the moment between breathing in and breathing out. Then lean your back on its chest and feel the beating of its heart. This peace, which is its gift to you, will give you incredible strength and a deep understanding of the meaning of life. Once you have achieved this, you can let go of all dogma and beliefs and be free – and it is in this freedom, this knowledge, that healing lies. When you let go of all negative elements, you will encounter God within you. The amethyst dragon teaches you not to suppress your negative side, but instead to observe and recognize it, and to surrender it. From its mouth it breathes a violet flame for you, challenging you to let go of all your negativity and commit it to this flame, in love and gratitude.

Close your eyes, take a few deep breaths and access a negative aspect within you, such as envy or your inner saboteur. Give form to this part of you, then take it in your arms like a baby and rock it to and fro lovingly.

Tell it that it is allowed to be, that you are aware of it and that it can now be free. Give this part of you to your dragon with all your love – the dragon will dispose of it so that what is now low can be transformed into what is high. Do the same with other negative thoughts as well, such as 'I'm too old', 'I won't find a partner, who would want me' and 'nobody loves me'. Free yourself from everything that brings you down and makes you small, from anything that drains your power and stops you shining.

Place yourself in the violet flame exhaled by your dragon so that it can burn away all your errors and tear down every barrier. Connect deeply with your dragon and feel the power of endless love, the freedom, the peace and the limitless consciousness. The most powerful magic is to be found in silence. Enlighten and refine your whole being, make your heart a place of peace and silence, so that you can hear the message of the divine source and share it with people.

This wonderful dragon will bring you deep peace and *joie de vivre*. It wants to help you find your spiritual partner. When all negative elements have been transformed, you will be ready to meet your spiritual partner and to recognise them as such. Spend a good deal of time near your amethyst dragon and become charged with its energy. The people around you will take note and approve, since it will give you an irresistible charisma. Take the violet light and the beauty into your aura.

The violet amethyst dragon will enable you to follow the path of the Buddha. It will accompany you and teach you that you must give up everything to receive everything. It will lead you to a learning of devotion and dedication and a knowledge of your true self.

THE PINK LOVE DRAGON

The love dragon is pink or rose-coloured, with scales that are mostly edged in white. Endowed with graceful beauty, it resembles an extraordinary piece of jewellery. And yet it is modest and would like to teach you that modesty, even though long ago you may have recognised that you are a great light in a human body. When the love dragon chooses you, it is time to remember – to remember when you were one of the followers of Jesus, The Christ. A time when you learned of Jesus yourself. Now is the time to remember what you discovered then, so that you can use it today for the common good. This silent dragon would like to lead you into the solitude of the wilderness so that you can find yourself and spend much time in prayer.

Conduct a meditation and travel with your pink dragon into the wilderness, into silence. Entirely consciously, open your crown chakra and your third eye. The pink dragon is anointed with the vibration and mysteries of the Essenes. It can awaken your extrasensory perception. Let its rose-coloured energy flow into your crown and forehead chakras. Feel how the pink light diffuses there. Feel this energy in the upper part of your head and let the light escape from you.

71

Extrasensory perception in all spheres – clairvoyance, clairaudience, clairkinesis. Let the sparkling pink light of your love dragon flow into all these areas – into your third eye, and the chakras of your ears and your hands. The light will become anchored there, with your will. Go on this journey often and renew the light until you achieve extrasensory perception.

This dragon would like you to be aware of your DNA, the double helix. When you see your DNA before your spiritual eye in the silence of prayer, you can change it with the might of the love dragon. If you perceive some damage in your DNA, send the pink love energy that your dragon has gifted to you to that exact spot and repair the damage. If you can do this in yourself, you can do it in others. Bring this healing to all those creatures who ask for it.

With the love dragon, you can also communicate via the pineal gland. Concentrate on that point, connect with your pineal gland and send out a golden-pink beam from your crown chakra to the crown chakra of your pink dragon. The love dragon requires that you recognise your potential. It requires that you learn unconditional love. It would like to teach you to enter your 'I AM consciousness'. This dragon loves silence; don't overburden it with many words but let love flow between your hearts. All that is really important is beyond the spoken word, contained in the silence and depths within you.

THE BLUE
UNIVERSE DRAGON

This dragon is large, but with a very slim frame. When the blue universe dragon chooses you, and when you are ready to accept it as your teacher, a significant part of your spiritual path will already be behind you. You are mindful and aware and the universe dragon would like to teach you to maintain the peace that spirituality has brought you. It wants the light within your heart to remain untouchable, whatever storm may rage outside. This blue dragon is linked with the Egyptian goddess Nut, the goddess of night.

Conduct a meditation and, on a night with a full moon, fly with this elegant dragon steed to Egypt. Land with it before the temple of the goddess Nut. Know that the temple of this goddess can only be seen on those days close to a full moon. Climb the steps before the temple. On each side of the entrance stands a sphinx. The sphinx on the left is shining in the moonlight, while that on the right is partially hidden in shadow. A blue light is shimmering from the interior of the temple. Enter and bow to Nut. Ask her to bless you so that you are a blessing. See what this wonderful goddess has in store for you, what she wants to share with you. Nut bears profound wisdom within her and from her you can learn all the mystical knowledge of the cosmos.

Nut is very fond of your dragon, you could even say they are friends. So you are now a friend and an ally to both of them. Fly often with your dragon to the goddess Nut on nights close to a full moon and let her teach you. Don't be afraid to approach her – ask her what you want to know. She knows that as a rider of the universe dragon a great task awaits you and she will help you to achieve it.

Your dragon's vibration is one of deep peace; it wants to pass this vibration on to you – peace in your thoughts, in your spirit, body and heart. Meditate and fly with your dragon into the universe. See all its complexity and beauty, just waiting to be discovered. Breathe in the peace that is to be found everywhere in the universe.

The universe dragon would like to show you other planets where you are to learn more. You will to learn to speak, you will learn to speak of peace, so that your word and your aura bring peace wherever you go. This is a great task. If you succeed, people will bow down before you – not out of fear but rather gratitude. The messenger who brings peace is a ruler, a true monarch. Say yes to your task and to the priesthood of a new age. With your blue dragon, you have a link with the spiritual world, with the divine source, and you can preach their messages to people. Let the knowledge that God is in all things vibrate deep within your heart. Recognise the beauty and joy in everything, follow your path and bring back the Golden Age.

THE BROWN TREE DRAGON

The tree dragon is brown or spotted brown and grey. It is a quiet dragon with an aura that is almost surly and morose; it is rather fussy and almost eccentric. If it is not in the right mood, it simply retires to a tree and sleeps, and then there is nothing you can do but wait. But it remains extremely alert – if something is wrong, it is ready in an instant. The brown tree dragon can sense bad situations straight away and urges you to distance yourself from these situations or from people who may do you harm. It watches over you. When you find yourself in need of its power to break with them, call the dragon to you and place it between you and those who wish you harm. They will sense it and retreat, although you must then also step back. The tree dragon will teach you how to withdraw but not how to go into battle – it is extremely peace loving. We humans have a tendency to make the same mistakes, again and again, over a long period of time. We are extremely stubborn and retain our old, harmful patterns of behaviour. When your dragon notices this, it will step back. It is patient and will wait until you are ready to progress and move on, until you are ready to see yourself. Initially, the tree dragon is very reserved, but once you have won its full trust, it will give you a great gift.

The tree dragon will unite you with the strength of Shiva, which is extraordinary in itself. You must be patient, as it may take some time. There is no point in trying to rush things – the dragon won't listen. This gentle and benevolent dragon is modest and urges you to be the same. It teaches that everything has its own time and season and that you cannot influence matters of fundamental importance. It is not you who decides if your heart beats or when it ceases to do so – everything has already been set down in the subtle records of the Akasha Chronicle. But when the day comes for your dragon to bring you before Shiva, you will both bathe in the god's amber light. It will then be clear from your aura that you follow the path of mastery, the mastery of duality. You will lead a life full of joy and ease – look forward to it. Prepare yourself well, practise some exercises to centre yourself.

Go into the forest with your tree dragon and choose a tree. Hug the tree and absorb its energy. Then find a tree stump and stand on it. The tree may no longer be there but its energy – its energetic essence – remains. Feel it, feel that you are standing in it and then centre yourself. Sense the power that flows through you, the steadfastness, the grounding. Go into the centre of your being, where all your energy is concentrated, where you are centered. Carry out this exercise for a while. When you are ready, meditate and fly to the temple of Shiva with your tree dragon. Shiva is the god of destruction and renewal. This energy separates you from everything that holds you back and is bad for you. This temple is not located in our world but in reality, in the tops of gigantic holy trees. The temple of Shiva is made from pure gold and is richly decorated. You will never have seen anything so beautiful in your life. Go to Shiva, and fall on your knees. Hold out your hands before you and ask for mercy and separation from all that prevents you from becoming the person that you are, or from living as you would like. Let go, let everything flow out of your hands, all the energetic slime, everything that weighs you down, give everything to Shiva. Your dragon teaches that ignorance is like a demon, don't give in to it. Trust your dragon, connect with it heart to heart. Follow and it will lead you to the teachers that you need. Learn. Knowledge is power. The peace within you will grow with your understanding. Take joy in this, as it will lead you to mastery.

THE CORAL DRAGON OF HAPPINESS

This shining dragon is always female. The coral dragon of happiness is extremely rare and only very few people have ever seen it. It brings happiness and joy into your home and creates a loving union between you, your family and friends. It heals any discord that may arise between you. This sensitive female dragon cries huge tears if arguments break out within the family – something it finds detestable. It would like to teach you that there is no right or wrong, it wants to teach you to forgive, especially yourself.

Conduct a meditation with the coral-coloured dragon of happiness. It will fly to the sea with you, but then be on your guard – it will slip into the ocean. On such journeys you are always in reality, far from the illusion in which we live and you can breathe there, even in the sea. It will glide through the ocean with you and the salt in the water will cleanse you. You will swim deeper and deeper, past coral reefs of beautiful hues and into a world of brilliant colours and bizarre shapes. You reach a crack in the reef, swim in-side and emerge into a dry cave, deep beneath the sea. You climb up out of the water. This cave is decorated from top to bottom with coral-coloured gemstones.

These stones glow and emit an energy that at intervals flashes across the cave from one side to the other, like electricity or coral-hued lightning. This cave is a miracle. Stand before one of its walls and gaze at the glittering coral gemstones. Open your mouth and let a bolt of lightning flow into you. Feel how the energy fills you completely and purifies you from within. You are cleansed of disappointment, abuse, unrequited love, shock and all that prevents you from being happy. Remain in the cave and absorb these cool, soothing bolts of lightning until you feel at ease. Go on this journey with your loving dragon as often as you need for it to do you good. The coral-coloured dragon loves to glide underneath schools of whales; look up and listen to their melancholy whale song.

You will learn that you are part of a family, but as a dragon rider you are also a high priestess or mage, allowing you to choose your family yourself and to take personal responsibility for your own life. As an exercise, the dragon would like to show you how you can free yourself from unnecessary and negative words and thoughts. Concentrate on this.

THE GREY MIST DRAGON

The grey or anthracite-coloured dragon is large, with a bulky and powerful body. It is a loyal companion that wants to lead you through the fog of emotions. Fog and mist derive from water, and water is the element of the West. Connect with this element and feel the power of the West. This is where the sun goes down and makes way for the night. The mist dragon is gentle and cautious. It wants to teach you to be just as circumspect, both with yourself and with others. Treat everything with great respect, for God is in everything. The mist dragon wants to bring you into contact with the light bearer, God's first creation. It grants you permission to work on the Merkaba of the light bearer. The Merkaba is a light field that surrounds our bodies; it is created by the counterpoised rotation of two stars – think of them as two conjoined pyramids of light that look like a star.

When the mist lies as dew on the crimson blossom of a rose, it is a beautiful sight. Stand in the centre of a room, light a white candle and listen to your favourite music, but softly, not at high volume. Visualise the image of the rose, look at the crimson flower and the sparkling dewdrop lying upon it, as if resting on velvet. See how the light of the rising sun is reflected in this drop of water. Take the feeling that you have right now into your heart, close your eyes and go back into your centre. Stay with the feeling, the vibration, and begin slowly to dance. A note will come to you with this movement – hum it softly. Keep dancing. See with your inner eye how your Merkaba is also moving to the dance. Feel how you are connected with your Merkaba. See the living Merkaba of the light bearer, how it spreads out, picking up the vibration of your Merkaba and itself begins to vibrate. Invite the Merkaba of the light bearer to dance. Dance together. See how the light bearer's Merkaba is beginning to free itself. It is casting off its paralysis, as if casting off old, heavy chains. Devotion lies in dance, sound is concealed in dance. Don't stop dancing; keep watching how the Merkaba vibrates through your dancing.

After the completion of the universe, the light bearer was God's first creation, and angels and humans are united in him. There are various accounts of what happened at that time but that is no longer important. What is important is that the light bearer is returning to his Merkaba, and he needs the rider of the mist dragon to do this. The mist dragon will lead you into the mysteries of the Merkaba, which is alive and has its own vibration. Ritual dance is a part of many cultures, just look at the Sufis, the dervishes. Watching these dances, you can feel the power concealed within them. All ignorance and error are banished with a dance of love and devotion.

Temple dancers enjoyed high renown in long-forgotten cultures, when their great task was well known. With their dancing, they drove away shadows and fear, and venerated the light, the sun and the moon.

The mist dragon also teaches trust. Imagine that you are standing amid mist and fog, unable to see anything. Many would be seized by panic, but the rider of the mist dragon learns that we have more than just the five senses and need fear nothing. We rely too much and give far too much of our energy to our physical eyes. Many have poor hearing or have little sense of taste left because too much energy is flowing to their eyes. The mist dragon wants to teach you that you can use your aura like a sense, too. Close your eyes often and feel your aura. Be aware that your work colleague who sits opposite you all day is sitting in your aura, as are the people in the metro, on the bus, at yoga or in a meditation group. Do you feel the difference? Let love – for yourself and for everyone – circulate through your aura as often as possible.

When your best friend is lying in your arms, crying, she will soon feel better thanks to the love flowing through your aura. Make this a daily exercise once people enter your aura regularly. Become aware of the sheer size of your aura and make a conscious effort to keep filling it with love.

THE LEOPARD DRAGON

This unusual dragon generally has black and yellow spots like a leopard, although they are also sometimes of different colours. The leopard dragon is smaller than most dragons but is still powerful and very muscular. When it moves, you can sense its profound wisdom. It is the most intelligent of all the dragons and would like to teach you to view your intelligence as a gift and not to let it waste away. Many spiritual people believe deep down that intelligence has something to do with ego. It is certainly true that your intellect will help you overcome your ego, as knowledge can only be transformed into wisdom with brilliant and crystal-clear understanding.

The leopard dragon is often seen with children and finds their hearts pure and intelligent. Jesus says: 'Become like children!' The leopard dragon wants to teach you to understand the meaning of this saying in the most basic and profound terms. As adults we can't go back or become children again.

Look into the eyes of your leopard dragon – they are especially large and bright. Look deep into them and try to see yourself within.

When you have looked into the eyes of your leopard dragon for long enough, you will fall into a trance. Let yourself fall, let all your thoughts drift. Be aware of them and allow them to drift like clouds across a blue sky. You are the blue sky. Nothing can touch the blue sky even if clouds gather. You are the blue sky, always there, always shining, always beautiful.

Bad weather or clouds may gather and clear. They have no permanence, for only the blue sky is eternal. Look into the eyes of your leopard dragon and sink into a deep trance. In its glistening eyes, the dragon shows you your life, how it was in the past or how it can be in the future. Always remember that as a dragon rider that there are several possibilities for the future. This means that you are ready to live your life taking responsibility for yourself. You are ready to stand up to everything you reject. In a deep trance, ask your dragon for the dogmatic beliefs within you that are preventing you from becoming the person that you really are. Write them down. Take a few days and read them through several times. Let the emotion that this produces within you grow; this emotion is power. When this power is strong enough, give in to the inner pressure and let the energy leave you. Shout out loudly that with the power of your dragon you are free of these dogmatic beliefs. Announce aloud to yourself that they will no longer be a hurdle on the path of your soul. Then burn the piece of paper on which you wrote down the beliefs, not in anger but in a spirit of celebration. Your leopard dragon wants to celebrate such occasions with you; it wants to free you, wants you to feel as light as a child.

It would like you to see the pointlessness inherent in success, in this desire to impress others, because it stems from the ego. Once you have recognised this, you can grow beyond it, you can be reborn and be like a child. Free yourself. Examine your actions. When do you do things to draw the attention of others to yourself, in which situations do you beg for love and only because you don't love yourself enough? Free yourself. This realisation brings liberation. And when you have freed yourself, look at the face of your dragon. You will see pure contentment there; nothing can make your leopard dragon happier than your liberation. And now you have been freed, go and free others.

THE STAR WANDERER
(THE COLOURFUL DRAGON)

This dragon is extremely large; it has small amounts of each of its colours, thereby uniting all vibrations. This dragon is not a spiritual companion and will come to you only as a power animal. This means that it will only accompany you for a certain amount of time – a week, a year or a millennium – but when it does come to you, the connection between you is profoundly intimate and charged with a great deal of trust. When a star wanderer enters your life, it indicates an ascension is about to take place: either your personal ascension or that of a planet. Look closely at the star wanderer and see what colour its chest is, then read the description of the relevant dragon and carry out the appropriate exercise. Then, see what colour its forehead is and again carry out the appropriate exercise.

It is a question of perfection, ennoblement and maturity. The star wanderer roams through space and time, through every universe. It appears only when its power is needed for an ascension and once that has been achieved, it continues on its way in order to lead others to light and love with its splendour.

OISIN, THE DRAGON KING

The dragon king is a tree dragon and is the oldest and largest dragon. No human may ride it; we must bow down before it. The dragon lives in seclusion in its cave and only a few initiates have ever seen it. The dragon king is wise and sends his dragons out to make contact with riders. He once sent a golden dragon to Uther Pendragon, high king of England and Wales and the father of Arthur. When Uther saw his sun dragon in the sky, he knew that he would rule as king over England. The sun dragon led him to his spiritual partner, and from this union Arthur was born, a story that is now well known. To demonstrate his gratitude, Uther had two great golden dragons created and made the dragon the emblem on his standard.

There are many such stories, and images of dragons adorn many banners and flags across the world. The elements of the Earth are subjects of the dragon king and his retinue, as all elements are combined within him. The power of earth, fire, wind and water are united within him. The dragon king was generous in his support of those kings and emperors who were pure of heart, but some were seduced by the power that had been granted them and misused it – the king of all the dragons then immediately took back the power he had given.

In the modern era, we have once more reached the point where we can become dragon riders ourselves. There will soon be no more kings and emperors. Everything is in flux; there are periods of abeyance and calm – we are all familiar with such times. The dragon king and his followers are rising and taking to the skies. Many of us are ready now or soon will be. It may sound rather like preparing for war, and indeed it is. It is a battle within us.

The dragon riders are going to war against fear. When fear has been overcome, only joy will be left – and then God will be within us. The dragon king wants you, the dragon riders, to find one another.

Close your eyes and see what the dragon king wants to show you. Breathe evenly and deeply and see how thousands upon thousands of dragon riders are flying through the skies. See yourself among them. Look to the right and see thousands of dragon riders, then to the left, and see thousands of dragon riders beside you there, too. Before you are the depths of space. See how a shadow flits towards you from the sun, how it is getting bigger and bigger. See how the king of all the dragons joins you. Free and riderless, he takes his place at the head of the army that fights in the service of love and that lets its loving power flow across the Earth from space. With a staff or a spear raised high in your hand to catch divine love like a lightning rod, you fly on your dragon to join them.

Divine love flows down into you from the sword or staff you have raised aloft. You open your heart and let this love flow down to Earth. Look again to left and right and see how thousands of dragon riders are doing the same. Take this image deep into your heart.

The dragon king speaks to you, saying: 'It's up to you whether this image becomes reality. Dragon riders who are incarnated in a male body, you are linked with the creative power of magic. All female dragon riders are blessed with the permeating power of love, you are anointed in the office of priestess. Pray every day and ask the spiritual beings for their blessing, so you too become a blessing. Each of you has been given a task in which you will be supported by your dragon. Know yourself and become the person that you really are. Recognise that you are a divine being who is now experiencing life as a mortal. Complete this and live your divine nature – now!'

Oisin, the king of all the dragons, lives on a small brown planet full of cliffs and deep ravines and where holy springs of sparkling, light-green water rise to the surface everywhere. Fascinating plants grow on this planet – blooms that shine from within or that emit a heavy, intoxicating scent. Knotted creepers hang down from the steep cliffs, while tiny white flowers sparkle like diamonds when light falls upon them. Here, in this mystic world, are butterflies the size of eagles. Let your dragon take you to Oisin, to the foot of the mountain on which Oisin lives, where you will be met by a unicorn who has come to fetch you. Take a strand of the unicorn's long white mane in your hand and follow this pure being. By touching the unicorn you are cleansed and prepared. Now is not the time to think – just feel and see what happens.

THE DRAGON KING AND
THE PHOENIX

The loyal companion of the dragon king is a phoenix. This phoenix is ancient, older than our mother, Lady Gaia, Once, long ago, it felt itself drawn to the pure heart of the dragon king and they became friends. The phoenix assists the dragon king, and therefore all dragons and their riders. In ancient Egypt, the phoenix was known as Benu. Benu is the bird of Ra, the sun god – it is a sunbird, a creature of the sun. The phoenix is very sensitive to equilibrium and truth. It urges the dragon riders to be humble and reminds us that every action, at whatever level, has consequences. If you should ever be hurt, the phoenix will be there for you. Call it and it will heal your wounds with a single tear. The dragon king respects the advice of the phoenix, as truth must always show itself in his presence and dark forces cannot withstand its fiery, penetrating gaze – they lose all their power. The phoenix is the friend and constant and loyal companion of the dragon king Oisin.

THE DRAGON KING AND THE UNICORN

Alongside the phoenix, the unicorn is a steadfast companion of the dragon king. As the purest of all beings, only the unicorn can take a human to the secret cave of the dragon king. The heart of this unicorn is linked to the heart of the dragon king. Made by elves, the path leading to the secret cave changes every seven hours and only pure hearts that are drawn to one another may show the unicorn the way. Those who are led to the dragon king must also undergo an initiation. At the entrance to the secret cave stands the dragon emerald. This great gemstone is some sixty centimetres wide and is embedded in a golden setting resembling a slingshot, which holds the green stone between the upper forks. To be initiated, you must place your hands on the emerald. A strong current of energy will then flow into your hand chakras. You will only be able to survive the force if you have previously touched the unicorn, since you this act will cleanse you.

The unicorns were also present when our Earth was created and stories about unicorns exist all over the world.

A unicorn's tear is capable of restoring to life people who have just died, and when a unicorn shines its light across a barren land, that land will become fertile once more. Unicorns are pure and full of light – but in my opinion, the word that describes them best is merciful. The unicorn would like to teach you mercy – to be merciful to yourself and to others.

ALBA THE DRAGON QUEEN

When you approach the dragon queen Alba, her light will blind you momentarily. Alba is as white as snow and every scale of her body bears a sparkling, shining diamond. She is sublime and incredibly beautiful. Her eyes are golden and surrounded by dark lashes. As the queen, no creature can ride her; she stands for liberty and love. On her head she bears the flower of life as a crown and in the centre of her chest she bears her own vibrating symbol, golden and full of light – a heart within a heart, with a six-pointed star at its centre, also known as a Star of David. The heart within a heart symbol is also known as the reverberating heart; it represents sound and the beginning of all things. The star represents the connection between all beings and the divine source. This symbol wants to show you your 'place', your vocation, the task of your soul.

This is the prophecy of the dragon queen: 'First you hear the cry of the falcon, then the cry of the condor, then the cry of the dragon. With their cries they worship the sun, and with their beating wings they spread the gospel of the spiritual world, and with their gaze they see into your heart. First the dragons will disappear behind the veil, then the condors will follow suit, but when the falcons disappear

behind the veil, it will no longer be possible to save this world as it is. So, awaken, ye people!'

Whenever the dragon queen appears, you hear a sound or soft noises vibrating within her aura. Just as with the dragon king, no human may ride the dragon queen; it would harm her aura and destroy the sound. As this sound is synchronous with the sounds in the Akasha Chronicle, it would lead to change within the Akasha Chronicle. For this reason, the dragon queen is protected by a small group of unusual dragon riders. These dragon riders have gathered to ride the pastel-coloured dragon that can be seen in the retinue of the dragon queen. These are the best riders: a dragon rider from the elven people, a dragon rider from the people of the dwarves, a dragon rider from the heavenly hosts of the angels, a dragon rider from the followers of Ashtar Sheran, who spreads peace and truth with his countless light ships and his retinue; one dragon rider is a scholar from Sirius and another is Master Surya, as ambassador of the risen masters. Six dragon riders of the seven rainbow dragons serve to protect the dragon queen. The seventh rainbow dragon has no rider at present – it flies alone with the others and awaits the next dragon rider from the human people, one who calls him or herself 'the best' and is also called that by others.

This dragon has been ridden by humans already and knows that once again, there will once again be a person who can ride it – one who will honour the last rider, Mother Mary, as a representative of the human people.

The snow-white dragon queen is covered with diamonds and sparkles as soon as light falls upon her. This glittering light combines with the soft sounds of her aura and emits an enigmatic, unique and delicate vibration. Anyone can absorb this vibration within themselves. It can not only pass through water, the element that our bodies consist of primarily, but it can reach far deeper into us. It penetrates deep into a cloud with every single atom centred around its core. This is its great secret: we principally consist of just this cloud. The fine vibration of the dragon queen expands throughout the entire galaxy and all those who ask for it are touched by it.

When the dragon queen speaks, you are momentarily overcome by dizziness as her vibration is so high. Her message to us is: 'Have no fear, we are with you. Be watchful at all times, as many confusing energies are trying to make you stray from the golden path of your soul. For this reason it is more important than ever that you are centred. Take care of yourself and your body. These confusing energies are cunning and conceal themselves everywhere, even in the food that you consume. Spend a great deal of time in the fresh air. I am Alba the dragon queen and I offer you my friendship. I send you my energy so that you can let the vibration of innocence shine into your deepest layers. My vibration is a vibration of freedom.'

A dragon king or queen is not elected, as we would elect a person or party to office; they achieve this position through right of birth. It is much simpler: they are what they are and have always been. In reality there is no time, and no reigns of monarchs or terms of office; everything just is. When you meet her, the dragon queen and her seven rainbow dragons, when you hear the delicate sounds, you will be overcome with such bliss and inner joy that tears will stream from your eyes.

Alba lives on the planet Lorién. This planet has long since undergone all its cycles of ascension, and love, peace and harmony reign there. Lorién can only be reached through a wormhole; you travel into another universe. Lorién is very similar to the Earth, but the proportions of earth and water are in equilibrium. There are no deserts on Lorién and no real mountains. The vegetation is thick, and there is much flora and fauna. Several elf cities exist on the planet, where some secrets are doubtless guarded.

I have thought long and hard about whether I should describe this in such detail, as in my workshops I have come to the unfortunate conclusion that there are still people who have no respect for the dragon queen. These people believe they are special and want to ride her without permission or enter her palace without an invitation. Such people are driven by their ego, they want to possess the queen and have her power for themselves. Personally, I find this alarming, as it places the whole planet in jeopardy and since these riders bring with them shadows from our world. But Alba, in her great love, is urging me; she would rather expose herself to the shame of disrespect than block the way for all those light-filled dragon riders who honour her and are ready to recognize her love – and so I bow to her wishes and trust Alba's eternal wisdom.

THE WELCOME ONE …

… is what my name, Arana, means. Wherever I knock on a door, I am asked in. Our cosmic or spiritual names are blessings and no coincidence, and your soul has asked for just this blessing.

The dragon king has welcomed me. He has watched over every day of my life and waited patiently for the right moment to send me my first dragon. The purpose of the red dragon was for me to become accustomed to it and I learnt so much from this wonderful creature.I now ride the black dragon with a fine golden harness and I am looking forward to my task. I am grateful for the experiences and knowledge that are granted me.

I often feel unsure and wonder whether I can write this and from where I gained the knowledge. I write about dragons, and perhaps only a few people will believe me and only a few will understand. But if I only succeed in bringing just a few dragons to their riders, it will have been worth it. When insecurity grows inside me, I close my eyes and go into the silence of my heart, and then I hear the cry of the dragons. They are coming to me, so that I can see them clearly.… Tears of emotion fall onto my black dress and the wind brushes my face – I am standing among them. I feel the weight of the sword at my hip and I am happy. I look up into the glittering eyes of countless dragons. In their gaze I recognize hope, they believe in us. Many are standing beside me, still without a rider, which casts a shadow across my heart. The king is among them and so I kneel down, ready for my oath. The words cross my lips as if I am dreaming and I know it is not the first time that I utter them: 'Great Mother, may your boundless love reign over all. Look down on me, I am your daughter. Today I enter your service. I will carry your love with all my strength, all my knowledge, and all my devotion to every being I encounter. In this age and in every age. In this dimension and in every dimension. In this world and in all other worlds. So may it come to pass. And so look down upon me, send me your blessing and your light, so that I may become a blessing. I shall never leave the path of my destiny, even in the darkest hour, this I swear upon my life. All my love, my loyalty, and all my strength are devoted to the service of love.'

We hope this little book of dragons will reach all those for whom it was written.

Arana & Black

AFTERWORD

The dragons would like to teach you to have courage, to achieve great things. They would also like to teach you that great deeds come at a price. The price is often that you must follow your path alone. Dragons are appearing more and more in our time, since they are the guardians of the great goddess – our Great Mother, Lady Gaia. She needs the dragons and she will need you, the courageous among you, those who are ready to mount their dragons and protect the weak. Come and serve the only true power: the power of love. We should remember that there has already been such a time, when love ruled our planet. Stonehenge and many other places of power were built to remind us of this time. The dragons want us to remember that we were all there in that time. Deep in our hearts, we know that it is possible – love and peace for every creature. May all feel at peace, be happy and free of fear.

113

ACKNOWLEDGEMENTS

… a word of thanks and the greatest appreciation! We would like to thank Anja Kostka from the bottom our hearts for the incredibly beautiful pictures. Anja has conjured into life the images for my texts and interpreted the individual topics for the cards with great feeling. Do place an order with Anja, should you be interested.

From heart to heart
Arana & Black

For more information about the artist, please go to:
www.anja-kostka.de

ABOUT THE AUTHOR

Christine Arana Fader was connected to the Spiritual World by dragon energy in 2000. For ten years, she was trained by light-filled beings and dragons before making her work public in 2010.

She has since become known for her dragon work and is thus now known to many as the 'dragon lady'. With great devotion and love, she acquaints people in her workshops with the energy of dragons and with Avalon, which she has also written about. In this way she is helping people to understand that everyone carries their own magic within themselves – that inner magic that may now be awakened for our new world.

For more information about the author, please go to: www.goldkamille.de

NOTES

This handy reference book explains how to find relief from headaches, colds and fear of flying, and will help you to cope with long car journeys or lengthy days at your computer, all with just a few reflex zone massage strokes. You'll never want to be without your helpful companion!

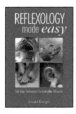

Ewald Kliegel
Reflexology Made Easy
Self-help Techniques for Everyday Ailments
Paperback, full colour throughout, 80 pages
ISBN 978-1-84409-666-4

There are so many occasions on which to send our best wishes to those close to us and choosing the correct stone gives those wishes added power and emphasis. This handy little book is fully illustrated with charming photographs and reveals the appropriate stone for each occasion and its message.

Michael Gienger
Crystal Gifts
How to choose the perfect crystal
for over 20 occasions
Paperback, full colour throughout, 96 pages
ISBN 978-1-84409-665-7

Healing Crystals is a comprehensive and up-to-date directory of 555 healing gemstones, presented in a practical and handy pocket guide format. In the revised edition of his bestseller, Michael Gienger, famous for his pioneering work in the field of crystal healing, describes the characteristics and healing powers of each crystal in a clear, concise and precise style, accompanied by four-colour photographs.

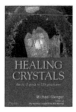

Michael Gienger
Healing Crystals
the A - Z guide to 555 gemstones, 2nd edition
Paperback, full colour throughout, 128 pages
ISBN 978-1-84409-647-3

This pocket pharmacy of healing stones embraces many applications. Although describing only twelve stones, the breadth of its scope resembles a home pharmacy. From allergies to toothache, you will find the right stone for every application. This handy little book offers you the essence of our modern knowledge of healing stones.

Michael Gienger
Twelve Essential Healing Crystals
Your first aid manual for preventing
and treating common ailments from
allergies to toochache
Paperback, full colour throughout, 64 pages
ISBN 978-1-84409-642-8

Tapping into children's seemingly inherent love of rocks, this accessible introduction to gemology provides youngsters with a base understanding of crystal qualities, the power of colors, and the metaphysical importance of positive thinking. Divided into seven sections, each chakra is explored and visualization exercises are included in order to experience the chakra's energy.

Ulrich Emil Duprée
Ho'oponopono
the Hawaiian forgiveness ritual as
the key to your life's fulfilment
Paperback, full colour throughout, 96 pages
ISBN 978-1-84409-597-1

This is an easy-to-use A-Z guide for treating many common ailments and illnesses with the help of crystal therapy. It includes a comprehensive colour appendix with photographs and short descriptions of each gemstone recommended.

Michael Gienger
The Healing Crystal First Aid Manual
A practical A to Z of common ailments
and illnesses and how they can be best
treated with crystal therapy
Paperback, with 16 colour plates 288 pages
ISBN 978-1-84409-084-6

For further information and to request a book catalogue contact:
Inner Traditions, One Park Street, Rochester, Vermont 05767

Earthdancer Books is an Inner Traditions imprint.
Phone: +1-800-246-8648, customerservice@innertraditions.com
www.earthdancerbooks.com • www.innertraditions.com

EARTHDANCER

AN INNER TRADITIONS IMPRINT